EARLY TOOLS and EQUIPMENT

by ELMER L. SMITH
Photography by MEL HORST

APPLIED ARTS PUBLISHERS

An Era Of Self-Sufficiency

Versatility rather than specialization stands out in the array of artifacts presented here. In the period portrayed, this innovative versatility was a necessary human attribute. Here are the tools and equipment around which a national characteristic emerged—the genius of a people for making articles that were useful and necessary.

Just a few centuries ago America was merely a wild continent richly endowed with raw materials. The pioneer settlers faced this fertile environment with limited facilities, but with a will for survival—demanding of themselves resourcefulness and flexibility. By necessity, every man was a jack-of-all-trades, for the pioneer was not only a tiller of the soil, he often had to be his own blacksmith, carpenter, cooper, butcher, tanner, and distiller. Independence was a sought-after goal and self-sufficiency and self-reliance were means to that end.

The early tools and equipment illustrated here have been collected since 1958 from barns and outbuildings in sections of Pennsylvania, Maryland, Virginia, West Virginia and North Carolina. This region, settled prior to the birth of the Republic, was one of the last to emerge from the era of self-sufficiency into that of specialization and industrialization.

These early farmsteads, particularly those isolated from main arteries of transportation, were typically representative of the early times and often retained remnants of the material culture of the past, including facilities for cobbling, smithing, coopering and distilling. Many of the tools were still available, although idle for many years.

Here, then, are found the last vestiges of early pre-industrial America as portrayed through its artifacts.

Contents

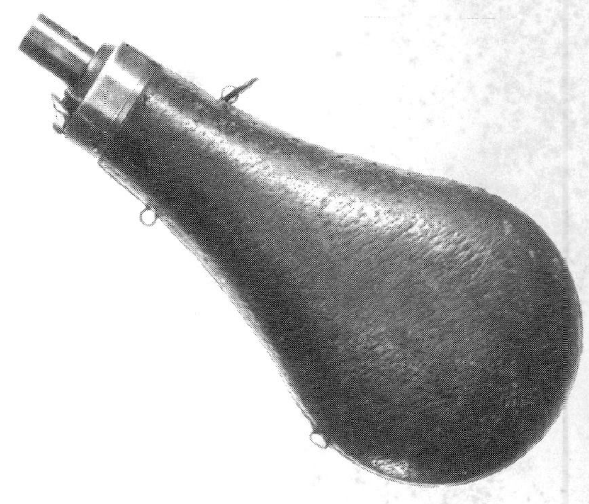

The ax, being the most significant early American implement, has been referred to as a symbol of American conquest; nevertheless, the axes used by earliest settlers were of European origin. These early tools were of iron but without a poll—the hammer opposite the blade—and the cutting edge was shaped in an arc.

The broad ax was used to rough out logs into beams, rafters, and trusses; it was not used in the felling of trees. The broad ax was made in a variety of sizes and shapes, with the handles usually quite short and often curved.

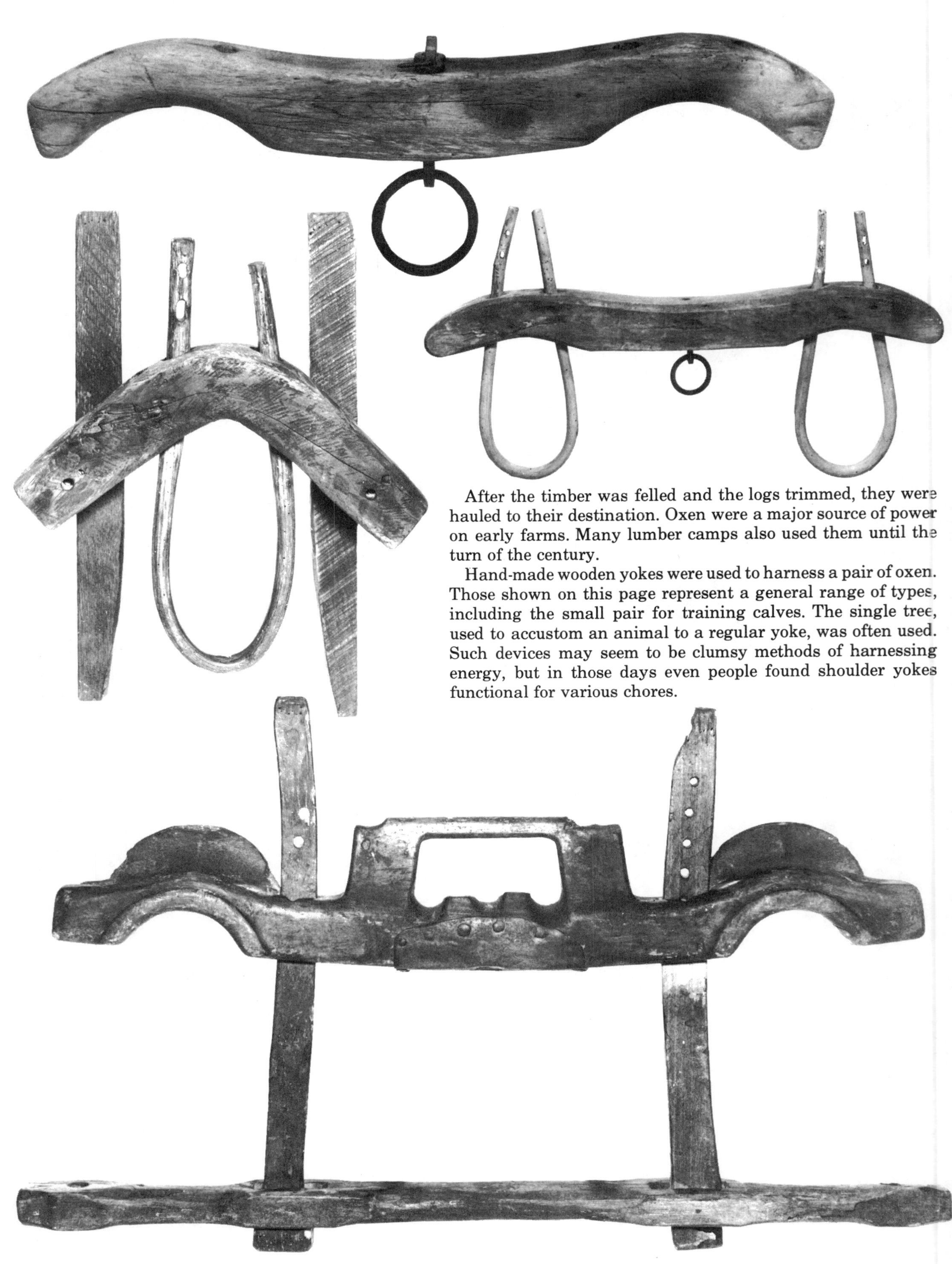

After the timber was felled and the logs trimmed, they were hauled to their destination. Oxen were a major source of power on early farms. Many lumber camps also used them until the turn of the century.

Hand-made wooden yokes were used to harness a pair of oxen. Those shown on this page represent a general range of types, including the small pair for training calves. The single tree, used to accustom an animal to a regular yoke, was often used. Such devices may seem to be clumsy methods of harnessing energy, but in those days even people found shoulder yokes functional for various chores.

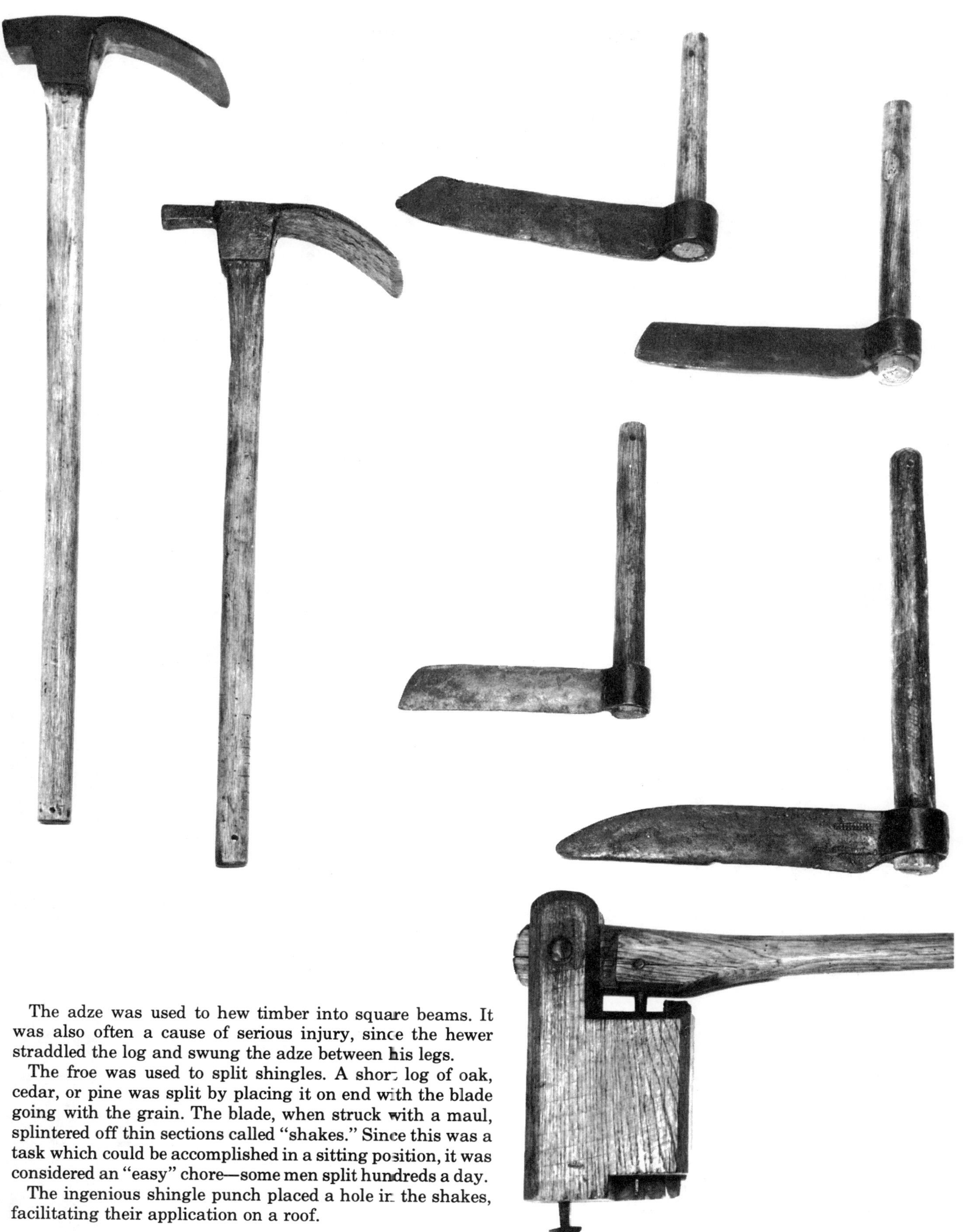

The adze was used to hew timber into square beams. It was also often a cause of serious injury, since the hewer straddled the log and swung the adze between his legs.

The froe was used to split shingles. A short log of oak, cedar, or pine was split by placing it on end with the blade going with the grain. The blade, when struck with a maul, splintered off thin sections called "shakes." Since this was a task which could be accomplished in a sitting position, it was considered an "easy" chore—some men split hundreds a day.

The ingenious shingle punch placed a hole in the shakes, facilitating their application on a roof.

The early log structures were made of hewn logs held together by mortised joints secured by wooden oak pegs called trunnels. The auger drilled the holes in heavy timbers for the insertion of these trunnels.

Although the wooden brace and bit was developed early, it could not serve for heavy construction. The auger was needed on thick beams requiring large diameter holes.

The bench or post bit was used to ream out long logs used as water pipes in many areas. Some of these wooden water pipes were still in service in a number of American communities at this late date!

Clearing the land was a hard task, demanding heavy equipment and a good deal of horse-power. The heavy root and stump chain was used to clear fields. The large specimen shown was hand-wrought by a Timberville, Virginia blacksmith. It weighs over a hundred pounds!

What early farm was without fence stretchers, bark peelers, and post hole drills? Few were quite as primitive, however, as this wrought-iron trimmed stump drill, which would challenge the strongest of men to lift.

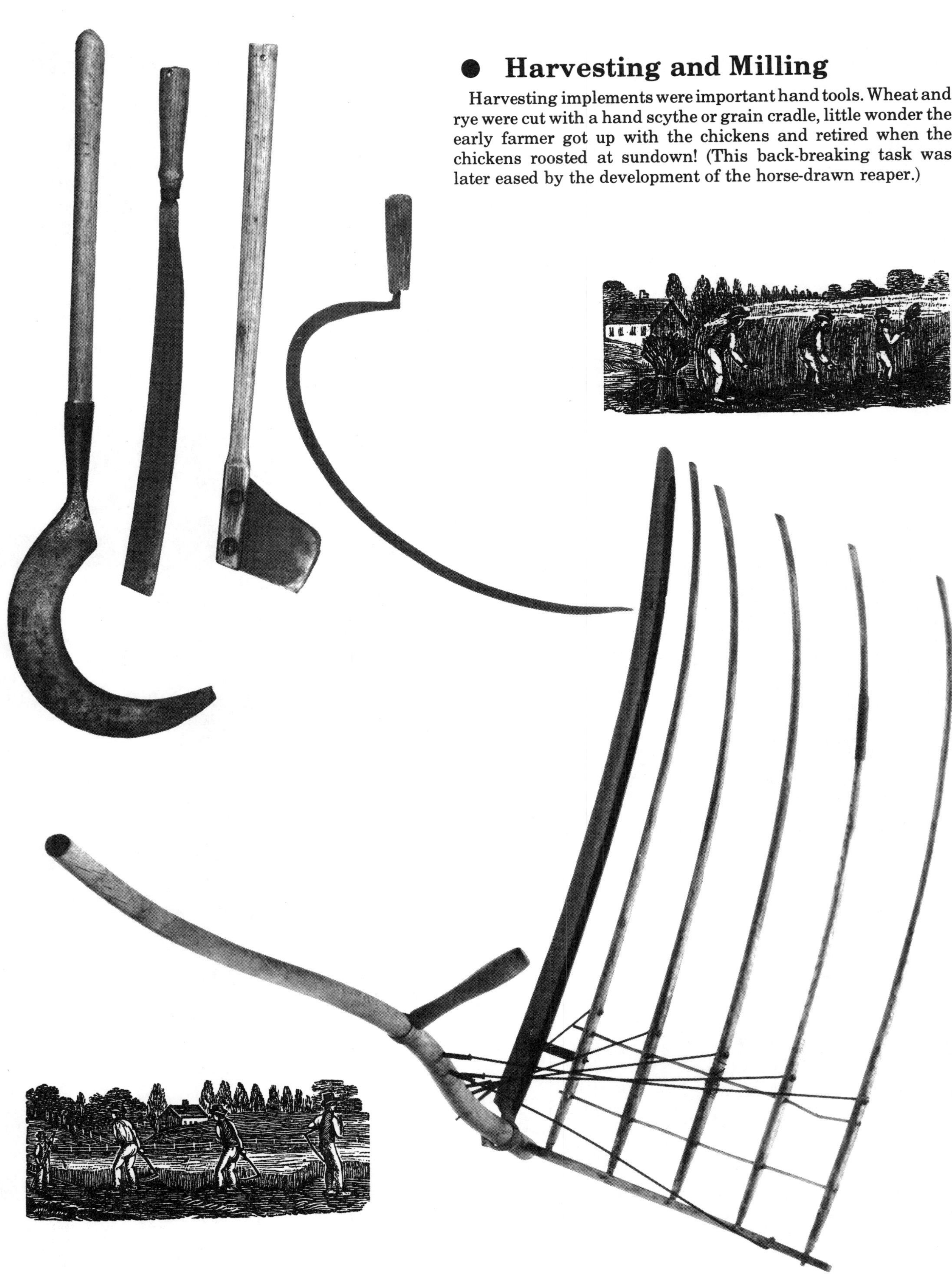

Harvesting and Milling

Harvesting implements were important hand tools. Wheat and rye were cut with a hand scythe or grain cradle, little wonder the early farmer got up with the chickens and retired when the chickens roosted at sundown! (This back-breaking task was later eased by the development of the horse-drawn reaper.)

Since grain was a staple crop used for cash, daily bread, feed, and distilling, there are a number of artifacts directly associated with it—flails, grain measures, wooden shovels and scoops, and similar objects.

The miller kept his records on a toll board which reminded him how much to charge or keep as his share for services rendered.

Every neighborhood had a grist mill. During the busy harvest season the stone had to be dressed quite often with special stone hammers.

The development of the horse collar facilitated the use of horse power and created a need for the specialized services of the harnessmaker who worked with leather.

The harness bench has some similarity to the cobbler bench and shaving bench; the vice-like device was controlled by the foot. (Earlier harness benches were without such luxuries.)

Jacks

The spring wagons and farm wagons were a means for getting in supplies and shipping surplus goods to market. Wheels often broke on unimproved, pock-marked roads, so the wheel jack was a necessary device. While the early wooden jacks were surprisingly sturdy, wrought iron bound oak lifts were used for the heavy freighters. The "Little Giant #10," made by the Ames Plow Co. was a late development used for light weight rigs. When a new wheel was needed, measurements were made with the circular device shown.

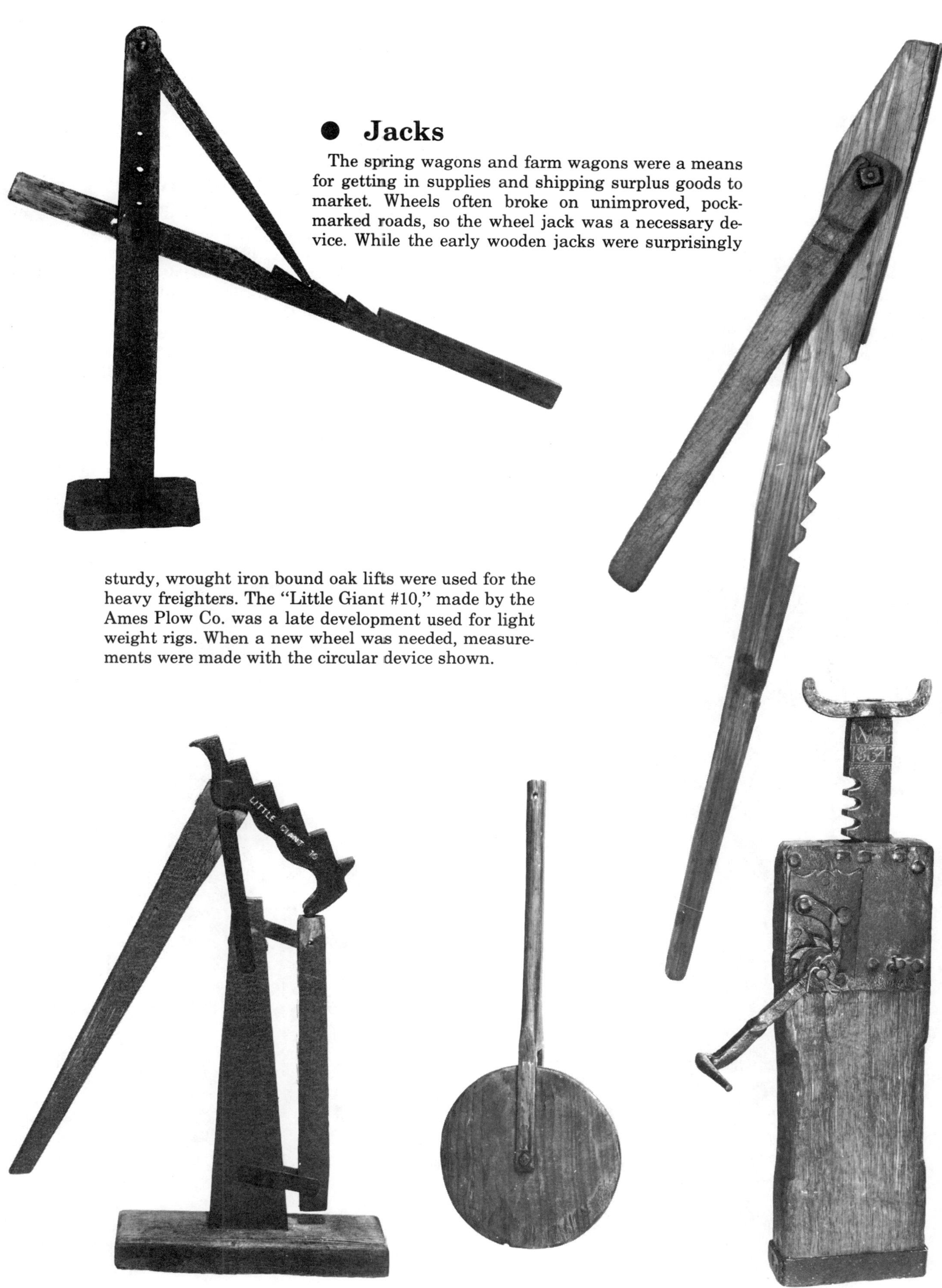

● Tools for the Forge

The early farm often had a small forge for repairing or creating ironware. These simple shops usually had a brick or stone forge, bellows, and a chimney. Here wagons were repaired, tools mended, and horses shod, until the welcome development of the village blacksmith—the smith becoming as important as the miller. The early mill and smithy often became the center for the emergence of village and town. The names of some attest to this today: Millville, Milford, Clifton Forge, Valley Forge, etc.

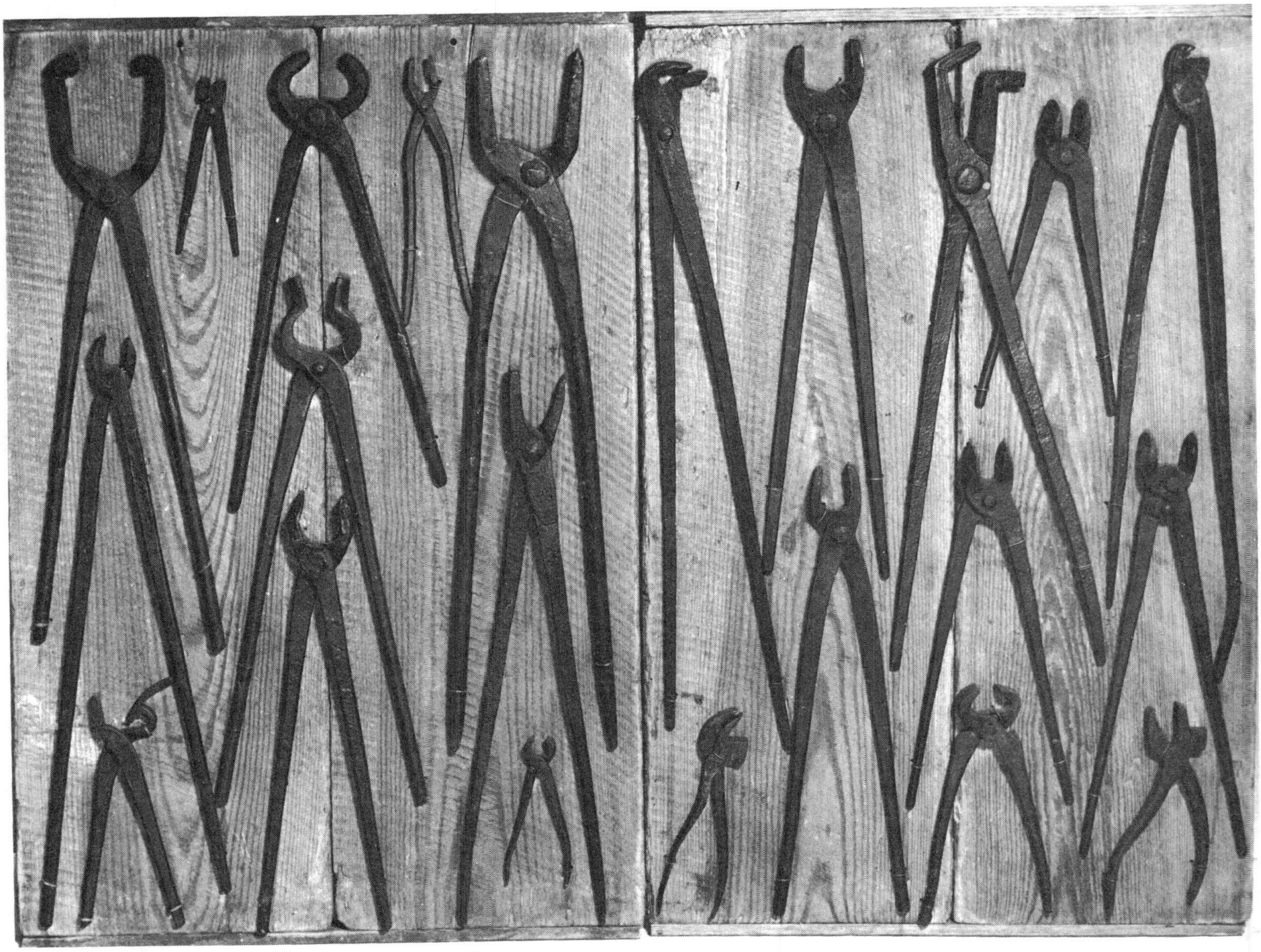

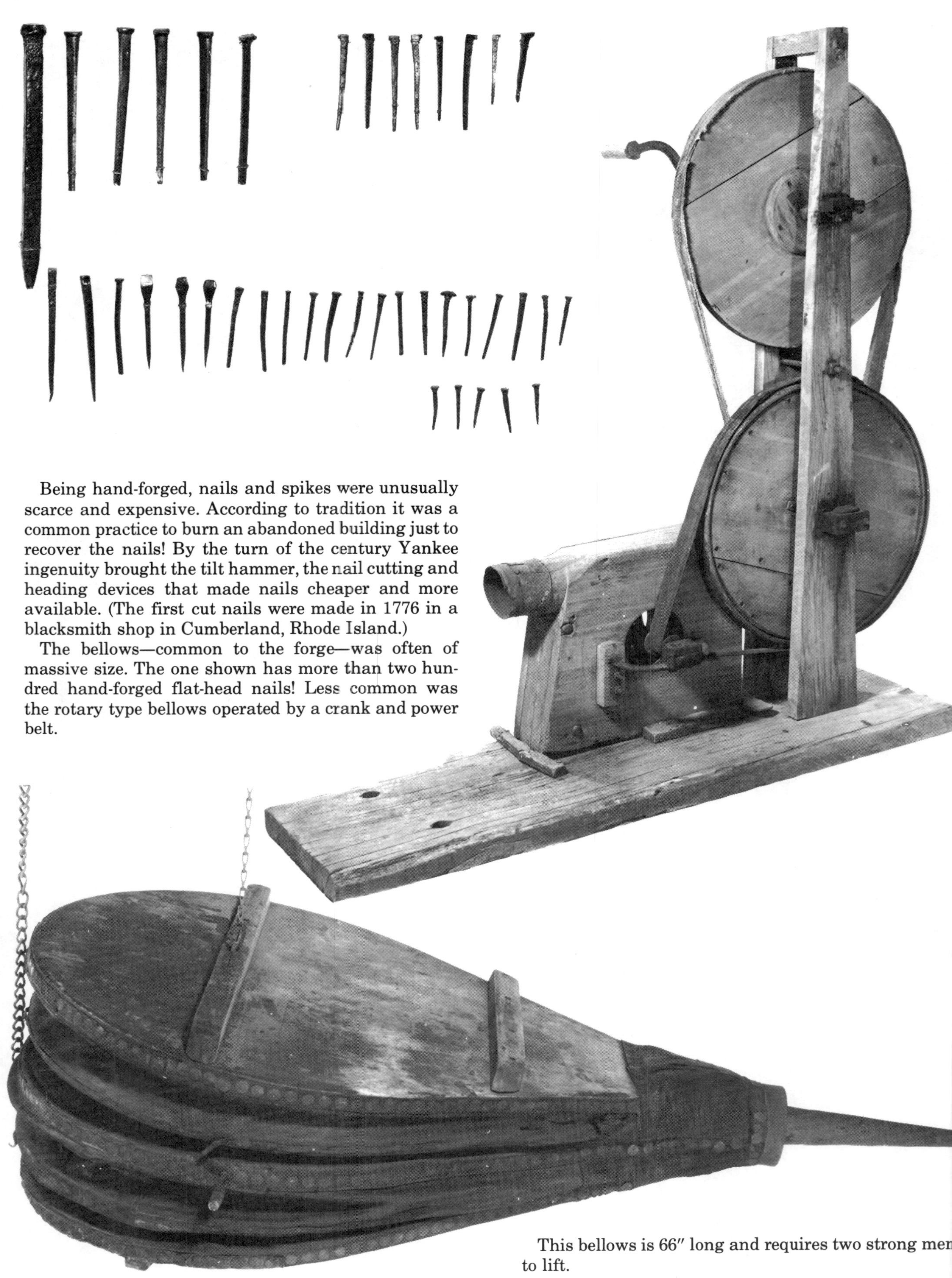

Being hand-forged, nails and spikes were unusually scarce and expensive. According to tradition it was a common practice to burn an abandoned building just to recover the nails! By the turn of the century Yankee ingenuity brought the tilt hammer, the nail cutting and heading devices that made nails cheaper and more available. (The first cut nails were made in 1776 in a blacksmith shop in Cumberland, Rhode Island.)

The bellows—common to the forge—was often of massive size. The one shown has more than two hundred hand-forged flat-head nails! Less common was the rotary type bellows operated by a crank and power belt.

This bellows is 66″ long and requires two strong men to lift.

● Shoes

Cobbling, another home task, occupied many evening hours during the winter months. While the women worked the spinning and flax wheels, the men were at the lasts making the family footgear.

Hand-made wooden lasts, ranging in size from infant boots to high boots, can be found in outbuildings on old isolated farmsteads along with cobbler stands, awls and hammers, and the pegs used to attach and join the leather soles. Such hand-made wear was durable, but crude and destructive to finished floors.

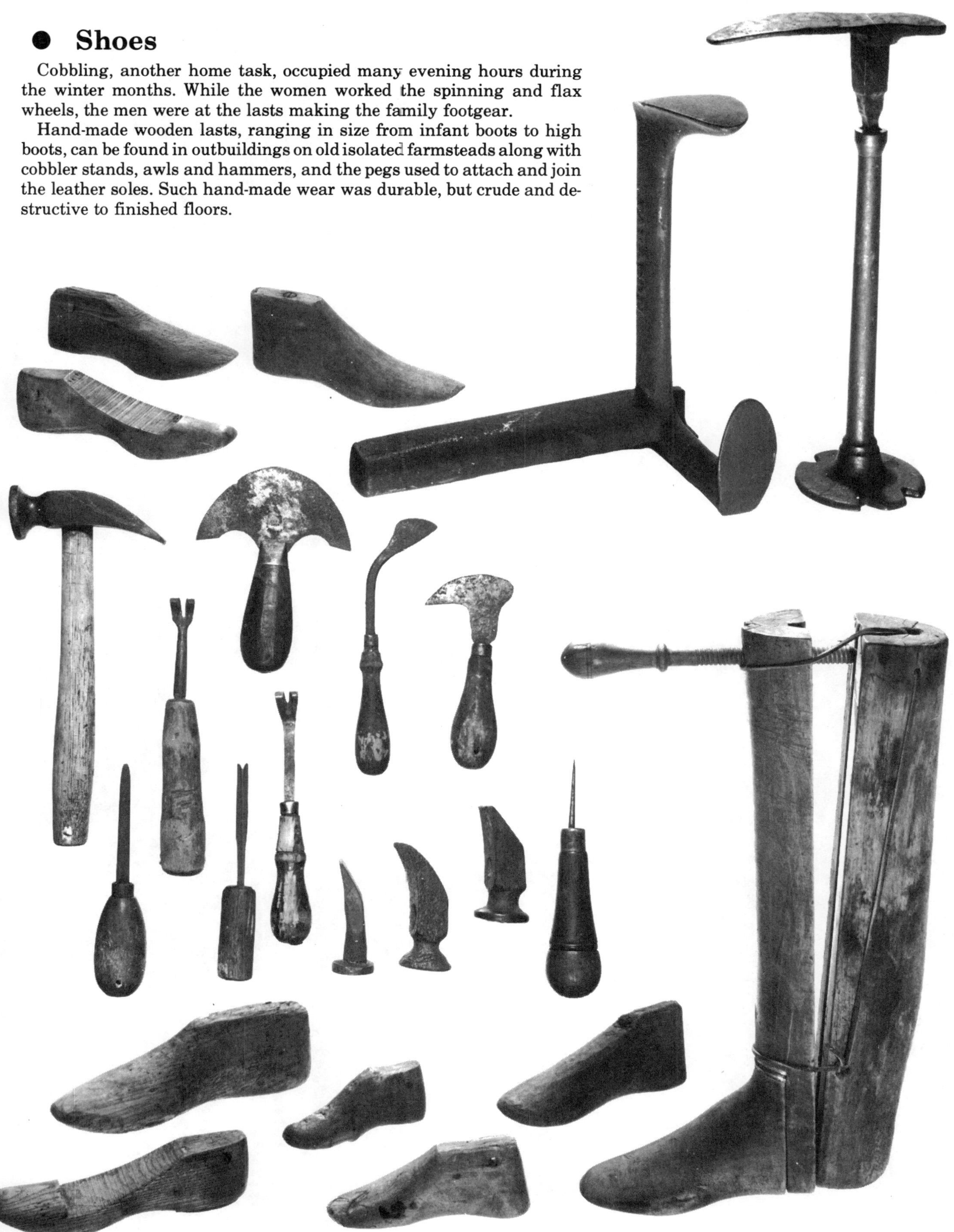

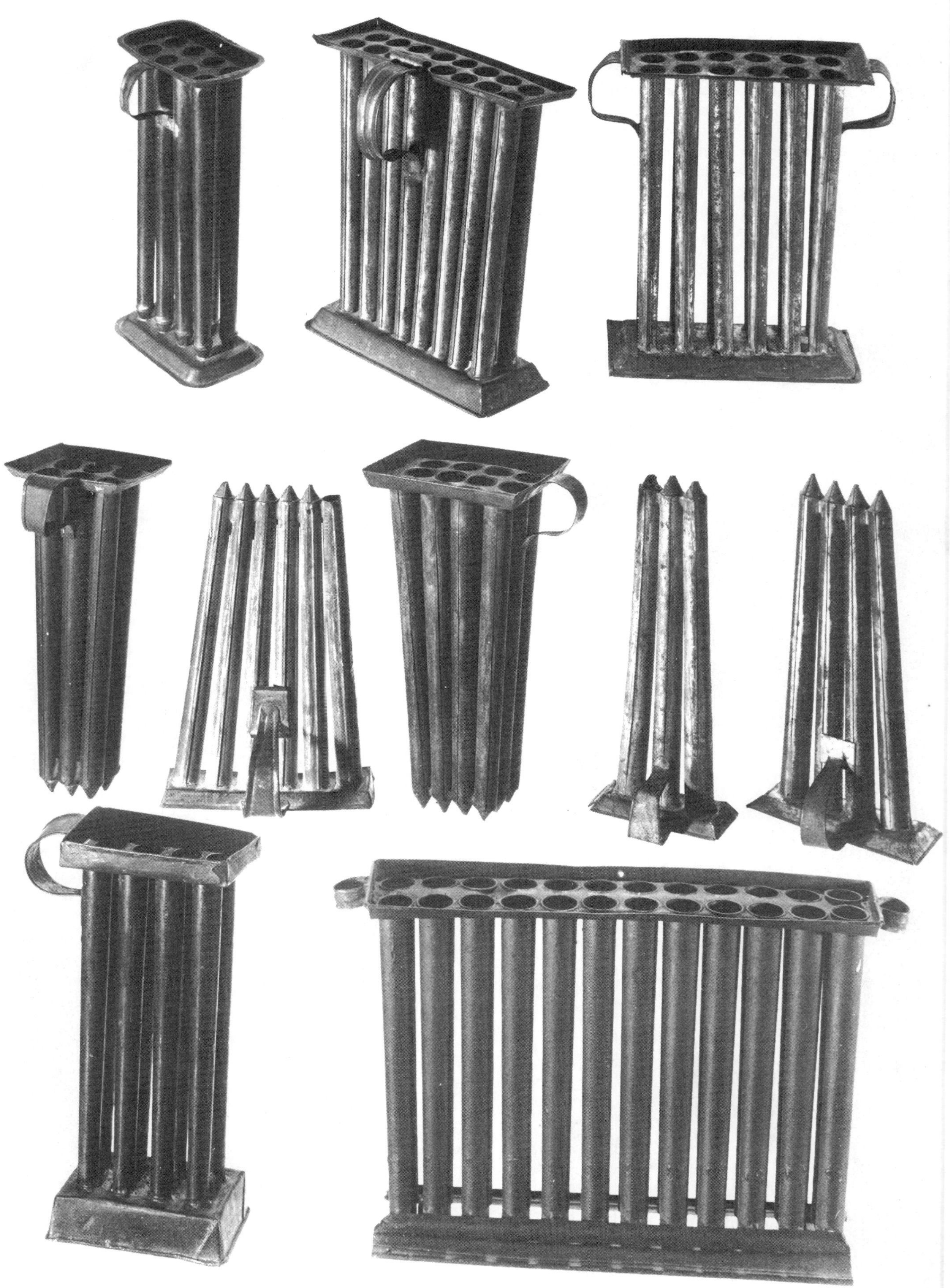

Lighting

Early lighting consisted of the rush light, betty lamp, kerosene lantern, and candle. Candles were made in the home from tallow or beeswax by dipping or by molding. The use of molds was common, being faster and more convenient than the time-consuming dipping required to form candles layer by layer.

Candle molds were made by the tinsmith in sizes from single-candle molds to as many as seventy-two to a frame. Artifacts closely associated with the candle include holders, snuffers, and wick cutters.

● Containers

Coopers, specialists in woodcraftsmanship, made containers for almost everything. The "tight" cooper made water-tight barrels and casks, whereas the "slack" cooper made containers to hold dry products such as flour, sugar, and meal.

The implements of the cooper were quite simple: various sized gauges to cut the grooves in barrel staves, shaving knives, hammers and assorted patterns for making the notches in hoops.

The shaving knife, referred to as a drawing knife because it was pulled toward the body, was a major tool. It was used both for smoothing the oak staves and also for trimming the hickory saplings used as hoops to bind together the barrels or casks.

The New World, with its vast virgin forests, offered a variety of woods for most of man's needs, but there was a demand for the products of the Old World specialists in wood. Although the farmer was usually capable of creating utensils, his containers were often crude, sometimes made from hollowed logs. Not only was there a need for wet and dry cooperage, but also for "shite" ware—referred to as treenware—such as boxes, bowls, churns, pails, scoops and similar objects.

The shaving horse or bench was used to smooth and trim shingles, peel strips of saplings for hoops, peel splint wood for baskets, and similar tasks. The clamp, known as a "dumbhead," was operated by the foot. A green sapling branch was sometimes attached to the clamp to pull the dumbhead back when the foot was released—a simple energy-saving device!

Baskets made from a variety of woods were in great demand as containers and for storage. But one of the most unique basket type was the rye straw basket, tightly woven from strands of rye coiled and bound.

The rye straw was wet, so it had to be run through a press to remove the excess moisture prior to binding. These were often home-made devices as shown below.

The large round basket was used to store dough while it was rising prior to baking. The small basket was used at the table for serving bread.

Rye straw press, hand-made and of early American vintage.

● Special Tools

Cow bells were made in some very large sizes. There were also sheep bells and, less commonly, turkey bells.

Nature was exploited to the fullest by the self-sufficient farmer—bees for sweetening, frogs were gigged, and cows, pigs, sheep, and in some areas turkeys, were turned loose to forage on the range or in the woods.

This is evidenced by gigs and branding irons (above) and bee smokers (left) and similar artifacts. Many of these implements were hand-forged, although others became available later at the general store or from mail order houses—but all reflect the ways of yesteryear.

Stone Cutting

In recent years there has been an awakening to the folk art in stone found in early grave yards. Although several publications focus attention on these designs of the early stone-carvers, the tools and equipment they used have been virtually ignored.

Actually, the stone-carvers used very different tools—chisels of various sizes, feathering devices of several weights, and hammers—yet with only these few steel implements they cut some unusually graceful letters and interesting designs on memorial markers as early as the Colonial period.

Fortunately there are several regional projects designed to preserve or record these remaining specimens of the craft which have thus far survived the ravages of nature, time, and human vandalism.

Few sets of stone-carving tools have survived the transition from the cold chisel to sand-blasting. The implements shown here were first used by W. Pirie and later by C. Woods. All were made more than a century ago.

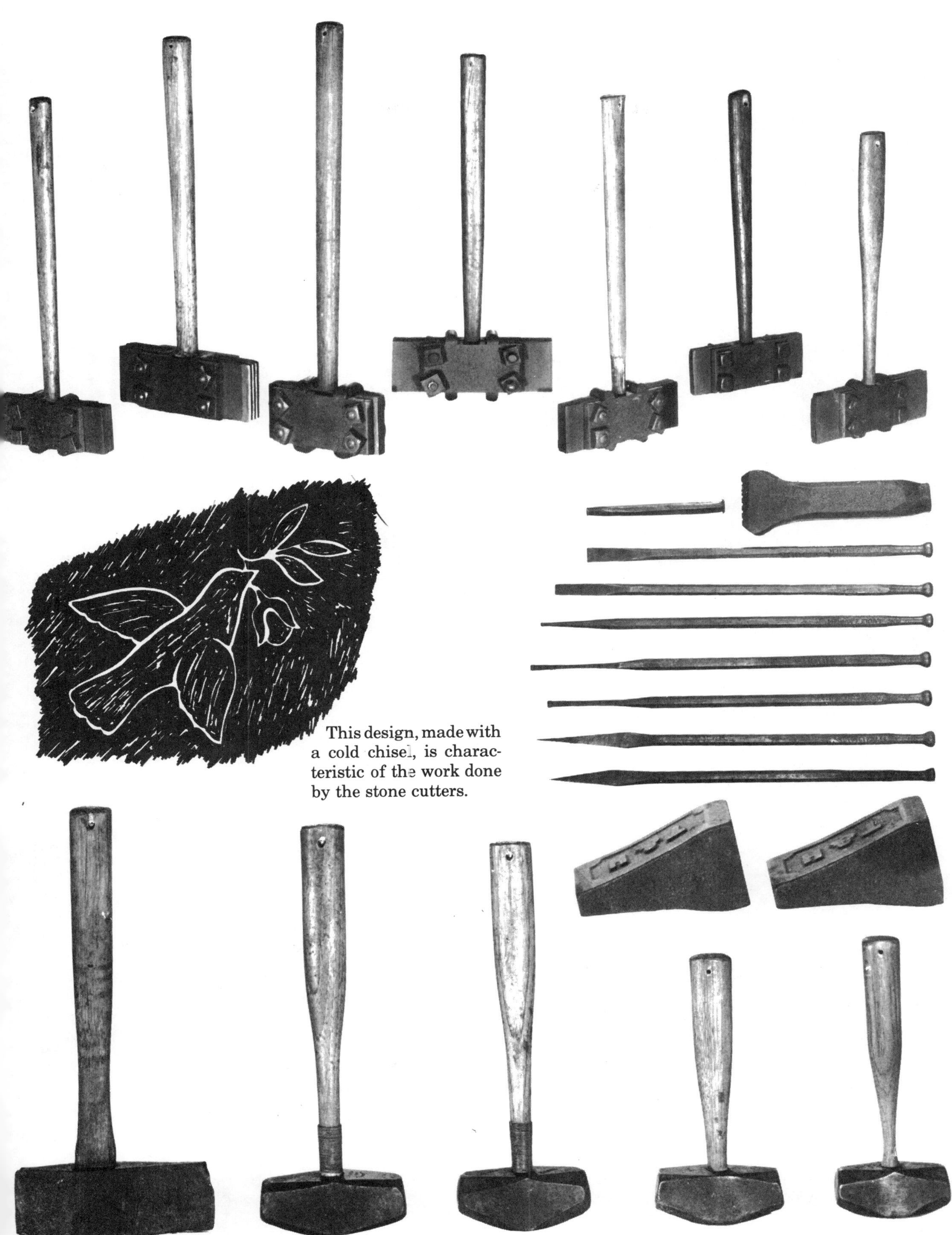

This design, made with a cold chisel, is characteristic of the work done by the stone cutters.

● Sweetening

The maple tree and the honey bee provided the only sweetening available to some early Americans. Many farms as far south as Virginia and West Virginia, harvested "tree molasses" from the maple grove during the late winter sugaring time.

Trees were tapped with a wooden spile, sap buckets were attached to catch the flow, the product was gathered by humans with wooden shoulderyokes and carted on ox-drawn sledges to the boiling kettles, where the sugar water was boiled down to syrup or into sugar cakes.

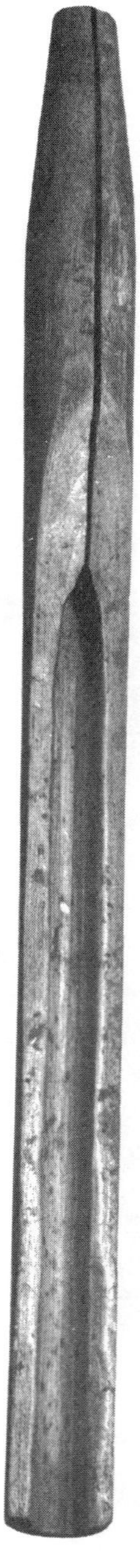

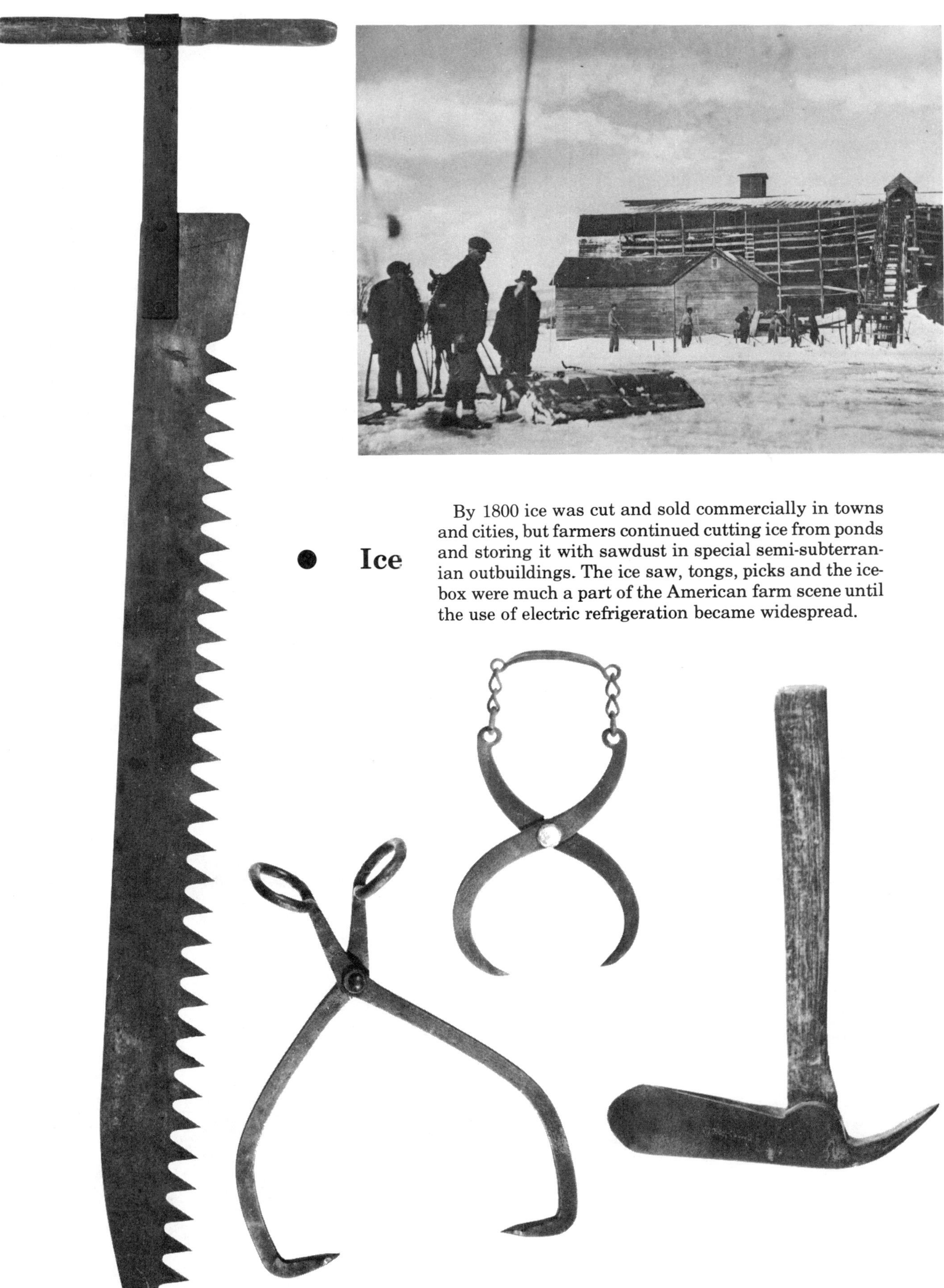

Ice

By 1800 ice was cut and sold commercially in towns and cities, but farmers continued cutting ice from ponds and storing it with sawdust in special semi-subterranian outbuildings. The ice saw, tongs, picks and the icebox were much a part of the American farm scene until the use of electric refrigeration became widespread.

The Tool Shed

The farm tool shed usually revealed some unique devices in addition to the usual tools needed for a wide range of tasks. Equipment was often available for making and repairing entire buildings or merely mending a plow share.

Wooden clamps were used in joining work. Board measuring devices were of many sizes, and there were small hand tools for measuring clapboards used in construction.

The spoke shaver cut rungs and spokes to fit into various sized round drilled holes for joining. This was one of the more intricate devices.

The hand tools on the right are hand-wrought pincers, nippers and tongs used by the farrier and blacksmith (except for the saddlers punch at the lower right).

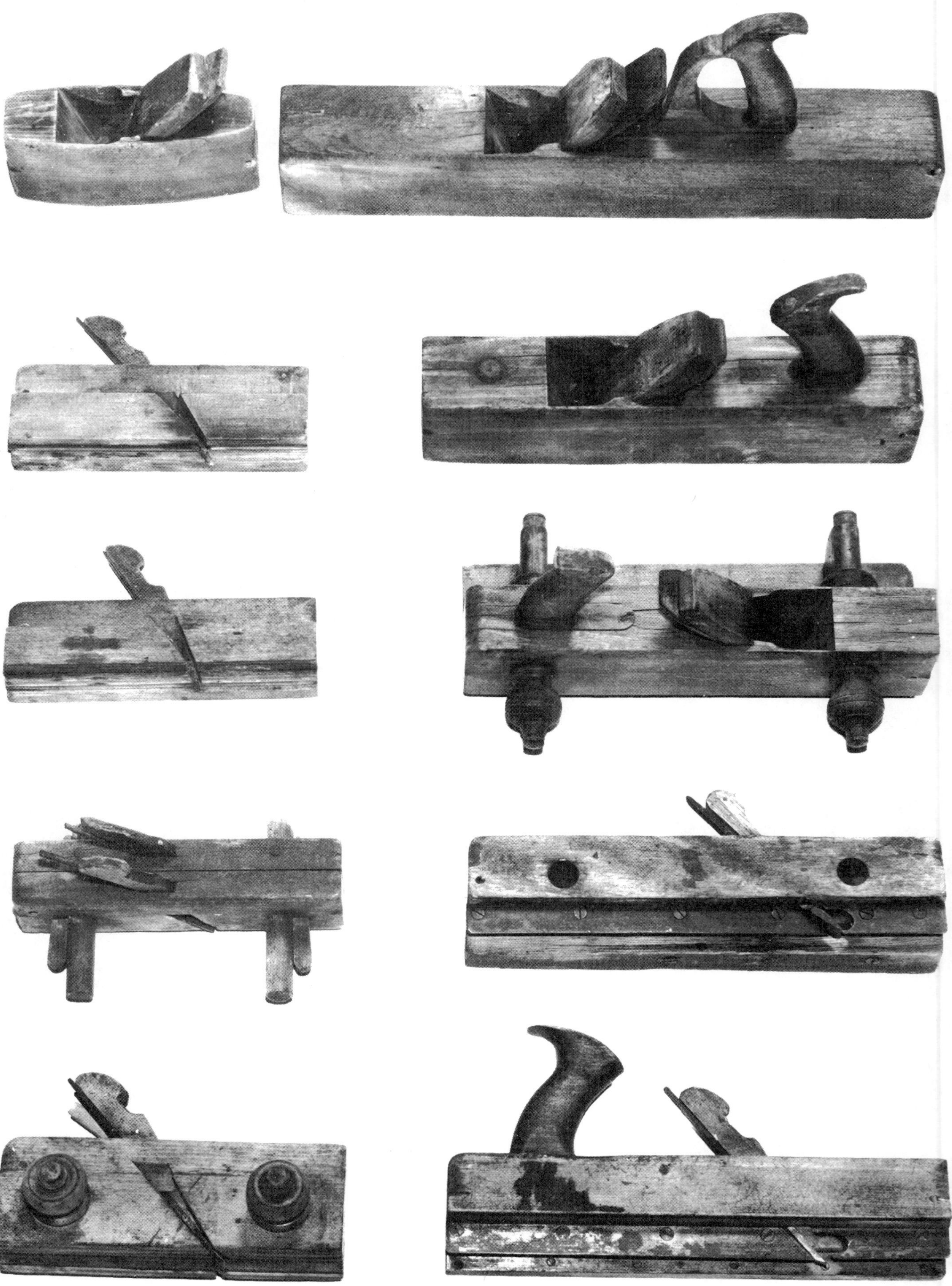

● Planes

The plane is an improvement on the drawing-knife. It is pushed away from the body rather than pulled toward it and far superior in workmanship. Planes were made of hard wood, walnut, maple, cherry, apple, and others, with an adjustable blade.

The large bridge-builder's type planes measured as much as a yard long and were therefore very heavy. Generally, planes can be separated into four basic types according to function: beading, beveling, molding, or smoothing. Although there are only four types, an early woodworking shop might have a hundred or more varieties for different uses!

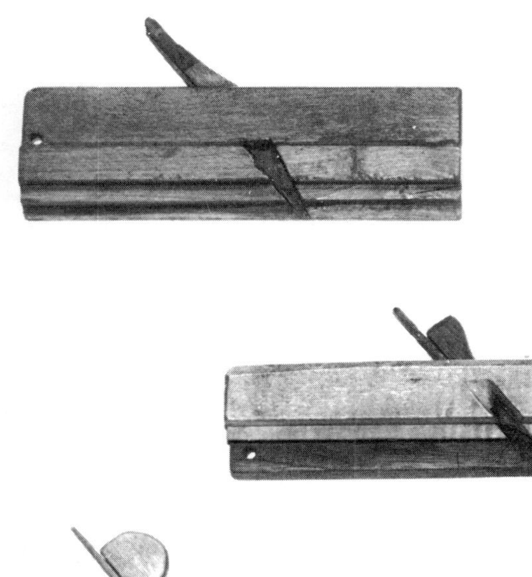

● Hammers

The top row consists of various types of blacksmith hammers; the center row shows (left to right) ball, spalling, shingling, lathing, and riveting hammers and hatchets. The bottom row portrays cobbler and blacksmith hammers (except for the upholsterer's hammer head, third from the bottom).

The two hammers in the upper center are used by slaters when installing a slate roof. They are flanked by (left) a brick hammer and (right) a drilling hammer.

The lower left includes mason and stone tools. Hatchets are (left) for lathing and (right) a broad hatchet similar but smaller than the ax.

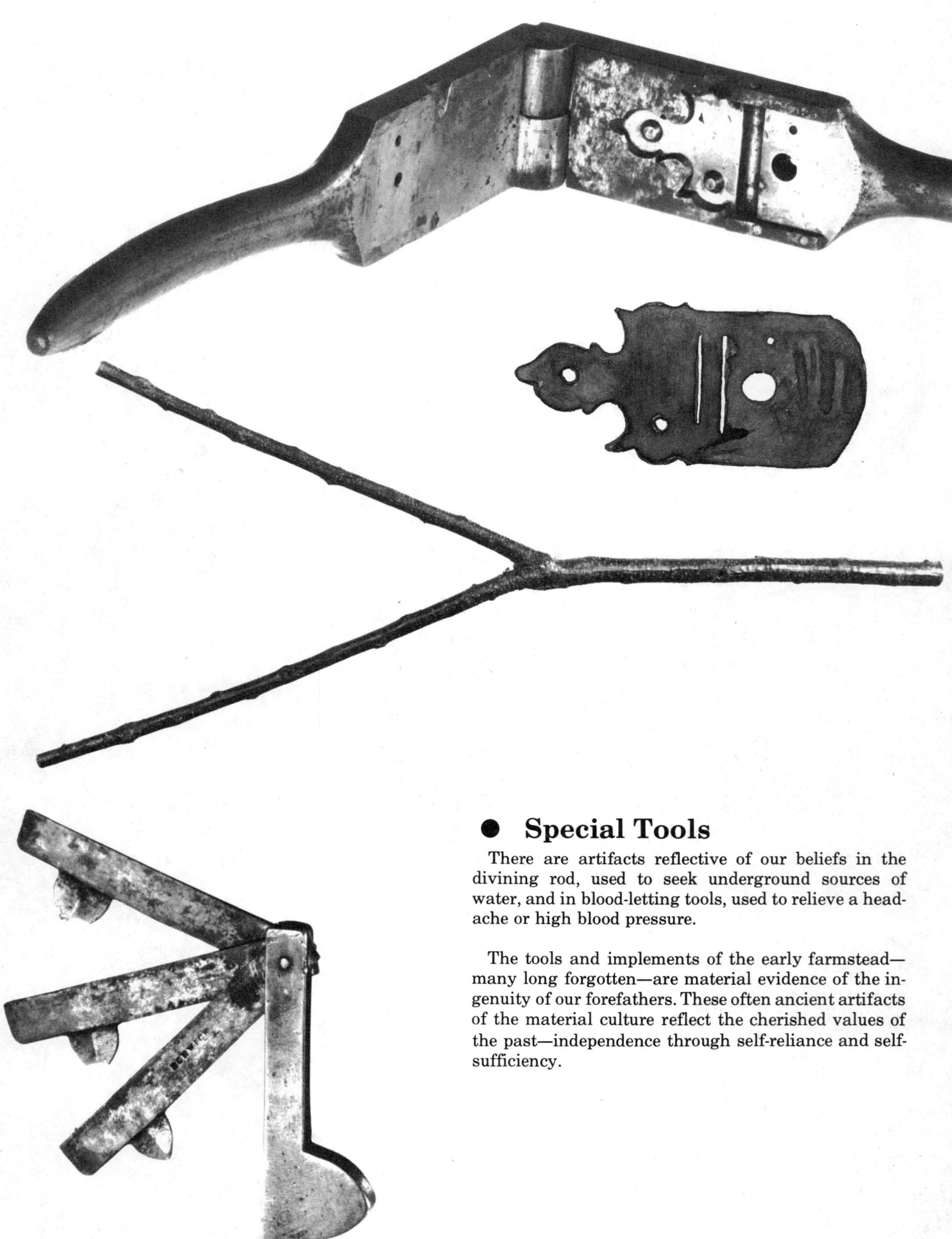

● Special Tools

There are artifacts reflective of our beliefs in the divining rod, used to seek underground sources of water, and in blood-letting tools, used to relieve a headache or high blood pressure.

The tools and implements of the early farmstead—many long forgotten—are material evidence of the ingenuity of our forefathers. These often ancient artifacts of the material culture reflect the cherished values of the past—independence through self-reliance and self-sufficiency.